PICCARD

© 1989 Franklin Watts

First published in the USA by
Franklin Watts Inc.
387 Park Avenue South
New York
NY 10016

US ISBN: 0-531-10727-2
Library of Congress Catalog
Card Number 89-5272

Series Editor
Norman Barrett

Designed by
K and Co

Photographs by
Action Plus

Technical Consultant
Richard Francis

The Picture World of
Motorcycles

C. J. Norman

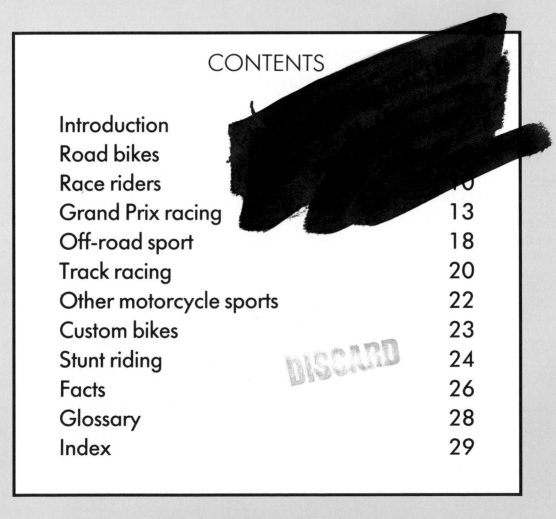

CONTENTS

Franklin Watts
London • New York • Sydney • Toronto

Introduction

People use motorcycles for sport and leisure and to get from place to place. There are many kinds of motorcycles, for riding in the city or country and for special purposes.

Police and messengers use motorcycles to get through busy city traffic. Many people enjoy touring on motorcycles. They use less fuel than cars and are cheaper to run.

△ Motorcycle racing is a popular sport. Cornering at high speed, the riders seem to lean over at an impossible angle.

▷ Motocross is another exciting motorcycle sport. Riders race around countryside courses on bikes with thin, knobbly tires.

▽ These members of the famous California Highway Patrol have very powerful bikes.

Road bikes

The power of a motorcycle depends on the size of its engine. This is measured in cubic centimeters, or "cc." Bikes range from about 50 to 1,000cc or more.

△ A 900 cc Kawasaki machine. This is a powerful road bike, capable of very high speeds. There are special events for "roadsters" like this.

△ Most of the controls and instruments of a motorcycle are mounted on the handlebars or between them. The fuel tank is at the bottom of the picture.

▷ A close-up of the front wheel. The large tube leading to the center of the wheel is one of the front forks. These are part of the suspension system. They have springs and a fluid inside to give a smooth ride.

Race riders

Motorcycle racing is an international sport. The top riders are highly paid sportsmen who take part in races all over the world. They ride for teams run by sponsors, who put money into the sport, or by motorcycle manufacturers.

   Success in the sport is a good advertisement for a motorcycle.

▽ The winning riders are driven around on a lap of honor at the end of an international meet.

△ A Suzuki rider is wheeled out by members of the team. The rider's leathers and his bike are covered with names of advertisers. These provide fuel, oil and tires, or put money into the sport in other ways.

▷ A rider's head is protected by a special crash helmet. Padding cushions his head and face and his eyes are shielded by a visor that comes down in front of his face.

11

▽ Extra pieces of protection that racing motorcyclists need are knee-pads for taking corners. They may lean over so far when cornering that their knee scrapes the ground.

The smooth tires on this racing bike are called "slicks." They are used only in dry weather. They provide more grip on the ground and help the bike to corner faster.

Grand Prix racing

The most important international races are called "Grand Prix." This is French for "big prize."

At a Grand Prix meet, there are races for various classes of motorcycle, from 80 cc upwards, and also for sidecars.

People enjoy watching Grand Prix racing, as the world's best riders pit their skills against each other.

▽ The riders line up on their marks for the start of a Grand Prix. These marks on the track are called the starting grid. Riders earn their places on the grid by their times at official practice, the fastest starting at the front.

◁ An 80 cc machine, the smallest Grand Prix class.

▷ The riders begin to spread out in the early stages of a 250 cc Grand Prix. Grand Prix are run over 20 or 30 laps (circuits) or more of the track. The sport is often known as road racing, because it used to take place on roads. Now, Grand Prix races are held on special circuits.

Racing is not just a matter of going flat out all the time. Riders must not overwork their engines, or they may not finish the race.

Grand Prix meets are held in many countries. There are world championships at each class.

Riders earn points for finishing in the first 10, from 15 for first place to 1 for tenth. The riders with the most points at the end of the season are world champions in their class.

◁ A rider falls off during a race. Spills do happen in motorcycle racing, but protective clothing and a safety helmet help to cushion the fall.

▽ Mechanics work on a bike during practice. Behind every Grand Prix rider is a team of mechanics and helpers.

△ In sidecar events, the passenger helps to balance the machine, leaning right out as it takes a corner. A Grand Prix sidecar "combination" is built in one piece and has three wheels.

▷ A rider and his machine flash across the finishing line in a blur as an official signals the end of the race with a checkered flag.

Off-road sport

Several popular forms of motorcycle sport take place over rough country or on specially prepared surfaces.

Off-road bikes have knobbly tires so they do not slip on loose materials or muddy surfaces. The engines are mounted higher than on road bikes to avoid damage.

△ In motorcycle trials, riders have to ride over tricky natural obstacles. They lose points for mistakes such as stopping or putting a foot on the ground. Trials bikes have special engines and gears that allow the riders to move very slowly without stopping.

▷ A motocross rider leaves the ground as he reaches the top of a hilly mound. Moto-cross races take place over several laps of a rough, hilly course. The sport has its own world championships.

◁ Supercross is a form of motocross held in a stadium. The course is built up from sand, dirt and other materials.

Track racing

Some motorcycle sports take place on oval tracks inside stadiums.

Speedway is an international sport. Four riders race around four laps of a cinder track. There is also a version of the sport on ice.

Other surfaces are also used for racing, including grass and dirt.

▽ Flat-track racing on dirt tracks is a popular sport. Ten or more riders take part in this kind of race.

△ Speedway riders use the left foot to balance their bikes as they take a bend. This is called broadsiding. The bikes have no brakes, and cornering on the tight oval tracks calls for great skill.

◁ Speedway on ice is popular in some parts of northern Europe and the United States. The bikes have spikes screwed into the tires for gripping the smooth track.

Other motorcycle sports

◁ Arena trials take place on an obstacle course built indoors or inside a stadium. As in outdoor trials, points are lost for mistakes.

▽ Drag racing is a contest between two highly powered bikes over a straight ¼-mile (402 meter) strip. The bikes, called dragsters, are steadied by a frame at the back. Races are over in a few seconds.

Custom bikes

Some motorcycle owners like rebuilding their bikes or adding special parts. This is called customizing.

◁ Very long front forks and a small front wheel have produced a "chopper."

▷ One of the world's most famous motorbikes, a Harley-Davidson, has become a fantasy in gleaming chrome.

Stunt riding

Motorcycles are ideal vehicles for performing stunts on. They can be ridden at fast and slow speeds and are easy to maneuver.

Stunt riders perform huge leaps on motorcycles or ride through fire. Teams of riders perform tricks and graceful balances on bikes. They also put on displays of formation riding.

▷ A daredevil stunt rider bursts through a wall of fire. This sort of stunt should never be attempted unless strictly supervised.

▽ The White Helmets display team forms a 21-person pyramid with six motorcycles.

The Wheelie King

Lifting the front wheel off the ground while moving is called a wheelie. It is not a difficult trick to do, but beginners should never try it at speed or without an instructor.

Some stunt riders can ride long distances on their rear wheel. Doug Domokos, who calls himself the "Wheelie King," set a world wheelie record of 233 km (145 miles) before he ran out of fuel. ran out of fuel.

△ Wheelie King Doug Domokos.

World titles

Italian rider Giacomo Agostini won a record 15 world motorcycle titles between 1966 and 1975. He won 8 at 500 cc and 7 at 350 cc, including five years when he won both titles.

The first rider to win the 500 cc championship and the new 250 cc title was Freddie Spencer, in 1985.

△ Freddie Spencer, double world motorcycle champion in 1985.

Isle of Man TT

The Isle of Man, between Great Britain and Ireland, is the home of motorcycle racing. The Tourist Trophy (TT) races are among the most famous of all motorcycling events, and fans travel from all over the world to watch them.

Riders in the Isle of Man TT race through town streets (below) and up and down mountain roads (above).

Lady riders

Motorcycle racing is chiefly a men's sport, but some women compete in sidecar racing as the passenger. Occasionally, a woman reaches the top rank in individual Grand Prix racing. Other forms of the sport where women have met with some success include speedway, trials and stunt riding.

Motorcycling first came to the little island in 1905, because of a law that banned the closing of roads on mainland Britain. The TT races have been held regularly since 1907. People still flock to the island for two weeks in June to see some of the world's best riders tackle the difficult mountain circuit.

△ Finnish rider Taru Rinne lines up with the men in a 125 cc Grand Prix.

▽ British rider Lisa Whiberley competes for the Essex Hammers team in the speedway league.

Glossary

Arena trials
Trials events on specially built obstacle courses.

cc
Cubic centimeters, or cc, is a measure of the size of an engine.

Combination
A motorcycle with sidecar.

Custom bike
A motorcycle that has been altered to give it a showy appearance.

Drag racing
A competition in which two special bikes called dragsters race over a short, straight course.

Grand Prix
A major international motorcycling event.

Grid
The marks on the track where riders line up for the start of a race.

Lap
One complete circuit of a track or course.

Leathers
A racing suit.

Motocross
A form of motorcycle sport that takes place on hilly, country courses.

Road racing
Motorcycle racing on road or similar circuits.

Slicks
Smooth racing tires.

Supercross
A form of motocross held in a stadium.

Trials
Events in which the course is split into sections and riders lose points for mistakes.

Visor
The "window" of a safety helmet.

Index